A collection of Design Pattern Interview Questions Solved in C++

Antonio Gulli

Design Patterns is the fourth of a series of 25 Chapters devoted to algorithms, problem solving, and C++ programming.

Antonio Gulli

ACKNOWLEDGMENTS

Thanks to Francesco Nidito for his code review

Contents

Design Patterns

Design Patterns are a collection of logical models adopted for solving recurrent problems which are observed during the process of software development. Patterns are not dealing with core algorithms adopted by the programs but are instead providing *reusable best practise* solutions for a modern software design. For this reason algorithms are essential for computational efficiency, and patterns are critical for building scalable architectural solutions.

In Object Oriented Programming Patterns typically show relationships and interactions between classes and objects. In this book we will discuss three classes of Design patterns:

1) Creational patterns, which create objects on your behalf rather than instantiating them directly.

2) Structural patterns, which compose interfaces by leveraging inheritance. The composition of objects allows to create new functionalities, simplify interfaces, adapt heterogeneous objects, improve performances and reduce complexity.

3) Behavioural patterns, which are used to describe interaction and communication among objects. Behavioural patterns are also used to handle the internal state and the internal activities of each object.

Design Patterns started to be adopted in Computer Science after the publication of the book *"Design Patterns: Elements of Reusable Object-Oriented Software"* by the so-called "Gang of Four" (Gamma et al.), Gamma, Erich; Richard Helm, Ralph Johnson, and John Vlissides (1995).

Creational Patterns

Creational patterns create objects on your behalf rather than instantiating them directly.

1. Implementing the Abstract factory pattern

Solution

The intuition behind an abstract factory pattern is to encapsulate a group of factories that have a common behaviour with no need of specifying their classes. This pattern allows to exchange concrete implementations with no need of changing the code that uses those implementations. This is because the factory typically returns an abstract pointer and the client does not care about internal details.

In this example the class Widget has a pure virtual method. The two classes derived by the Widget are implementing a specific *draw()* behaviour. In this illustrative situation we just print a different text.

Code

```cpp
namespace Abstract_Factory{

    // The Factory pattern suggests defining a
    // creation services interface in a Factory
    // base class, and implementing each "platform"
    // in a separate Factory derived class.

    class Widget{

    public:
        virtual void draw() = 0; // make it pure virtual

    };

    class OSX_Button : public Widget{

    public:
        void draw() {
            std::cout << "\tOSX buttom" << std::endl;
        }
    };
```

```cpp
    class Windows_Button : public Widget{

    public:
        void draw() {
            std::cout << "\tWindows buttom" << std::endl;
        }
    };
};   // end Abstract Factory

void testAbstractFactory(){

    using namespace Creational_Patterns::Abstract_Factory;

    Widget * w = new OSX_Button();
    w->draw();
    delete w;
}
```

2. Implementing the Builder pattern

Solution

The builder aims at separating the construction of complex objects from their representation. Instead of using different constructors, the pattern defines a single object: the builder. This object builds the desired object step-by-step according to the configuration parameters defined by the user. The Builder is different from the Abstract factory because the former delegates the construction of the actual object to a specific auxiliary class/object, while the latter uses inheritance for exchanging concrete implementations.

In this example the class Builder is implemented according to a pure virtual method *configure* which is defined in each subclass for setting up the parameters used to drive each subclass building process. A set of specific tests based on different conditions can be added to the skeleton code for driving the specific action items taken by the 'Simple Builder' and by the 'Advanced Builder' respectively.

Code

```cpp
namespace Builder{

    // Separate the construction of a complex object from its
    // representation so that the same construction process
```

```cpp
// can create different representations.

class Build{      // base class

public:
    virtual void configure() = 0;

    // here can add methods to see the internal state

protected:
    int configuration_1_;  // all the confs variable
    int configuration_2_;  // all the confs variable
    //...
    int configuration_n_;  // all the confs variable

};

class SimpleBuilder : public Build { // a derived class

public:
    SimpleBuilder()
    {
    // here you can add explicit tests on configuration
    // parameters for driving the 'simple builder'
    // creation steps
        std::cout << "\tSimple Builder" << std::endl;
    };
    void configure()
    {
    // here you can add additional configuration steps
    };
};

class AdvancedBuilder : public Build { // a derived class

public:
    AdvancedBuilder()
    {
    // here you can add explicit tests on configuration
    // parameters for driving the 'advanced builder'
    // creation steps
        std::cout << "\tAdvanced Builder" << std::endl;
    };
    void configure()
    {
    // here you can add additional configuration steps
    };
};
```

```cpp
    // the class that use multiple builders
    class ClientClass{

    public:
        ClientClass(Build * builder) : builder_(builder){};

    private:
        Build * builder_;     // stores the specific builder
    };
}; // end Builder

void testBuilder(){

    using namespace Creational_Patterns::Builder;
    Build * builder = new AdvancedBuilder();
    Client c(builder);
    delete builder;
}
```

3. Implementing the Factory pattern

Solution

The factory method uses factories for creating objects with no explicit need of identifying the exact class of object that will be created. Typically the factory pattern leverages the inheritance mechanism with the actual creation process delegated to subclasses. Factory is frequently used for avoiding duplication of code and for abstracting common functionalities. In this sense a superclass specifies generic behaviours by using pure virtual placeholders for creation steps. Then the superclass delegates the creation details to subclasses that are supplied by the client.

Factory patterns can be seen as a simplified version of an Abstract Factory pattern. The Factory Method pattern is responsible of creating products that belong to one family, while the Abstract Factory pattern deals with multiple families of products. For example, with the Factory method you can produce implementations (say *SUV, Station Wagons, Convertibles, ..*) of one specific interface (say *IAutomobile*), while with the Abstract Factory method you can produce implementations of a particular Factory interface (say all the type of automobiles given a family of vehicles including cars, trucks, caravan, and so on and so forth).

In this example we have one base class and two derived classes A and B which can be selected for exchanging the implementation according to specific needs. The only difference with the example provided at page 10 is that OSX_Button and Windows_Button represent a particular Factory interface for the specific operative system within the families of generic buttons.

Code

```cpp
namespace Factory_Method{

    // Define an interface for creating an object,
    // but let subclasses decide which class to instantiate.
    // Factory Method lets a class defer instantiation to
    // subclasses.
    //
    // Factory Method can return the same instance multiple
    // times, or can return a subclass rather than an object
    // of that exact type.

    class Base{

    public:
        virtual void what_to_do() = 0;

    };

    class A : public Base{
    public:
        A() { std::cout << "\tClass A" << std::endl; }
        void what_to_do() { };

    };

    class B : public Base{
    public:
        B() { std::cout << "\tClass B" << std::endl; }
        void what_to_do() { };

    };
}; // end Factory Method

void testFactoryMethod(){

    using namespace Creational_Patterns::Factory_Method;
```

```cpp
    Base * b = new A();
    b->what_to_do();
    delete b;
    b = new B();
    b->what_to_do();
    delete b;
}
```

4. Implementing the Prototype pattern

Solution

The prototype pattern creates a prototypical instance which is then cloned for producing new objects. This pattern is very effective when the cost of cloning is less than the cost of creating a new object.

In this example we define a class Proto with a protected virtual method *clone()* which must be implemented by the subclasses. Different prototypes are stored in a static array and the subclasses have to register themselves.

Code

```cpp
namespace Prototype{

    // Specify the kinds of objects to create using a
    // prototypical instance, and create new objects
    // by copying this prototype.

    // Declare an abstract base class that specifies a
    // pure virtual "clone" method, and, maintains a
    // dictionary of all "cloneable" concrete derived
    // classes.

    class Base {
    public:
        virtual Base* clone() = 0;
        virtual void doSomething() = 0;
    };

    class Factory {
    public:
        static Base* makeBase(int choice);
    private:
        static Base* s_prototypes[3];
    };
```

```cpp
class A : public Base{
public:
    Base*   clone() { return new A; }
    void doSomething() {
        std::cout << "A is now doing\n";
    }
};

class B : public Base {
public:
    Base*   clone() { return new B; }
    void doSomething() {
        std::cout << "B is now doing\n";
    }
};

Base* Factory::s_prototypes[] = {
    0, new A, new B
};
Base* Factory::makeBase(int choice) {
    return s_prototypes[choice]->clone();
}
// end Protype
};

void testPrototype(){

    using namespace Creational_Patterns::Prototype;
    Base * b = Factory::makeBase(1);
    b->doSomething();
    delete b;
}
```

5. Implementing the Singleton pattern

Solution

This pattern restricts the instantiation of a class to one single object. In a single thread environment the constructor is typically private and a *static* instance is initialized only once by checking its nullness.

Code

```cpp
namespace Singleton{

    // Ensure a class has only one instance,
```

```
// and provide a global point of access to it.

// The singleton pattern must be carefully constructed
// in multi-threaded applications.
// The classic solution to this problem is to use mutual
// exclusion on the class that indicates that the object
// is being instantiated.

class Single{

public:
    static Single * getInstance(void) {
        if (!instance_){
            instance_ = new Single();
        }
        return instance_;
    };

private:
    // cannot be invoked
    Single(){ std::cout << "\tSingle" << std::endl; };

    static Single * instance_;  // a single instance
};

Single *Single::instance_;  // force instantiation

}; // end Singleton


void testSingleton(){

    using namespace Creational_Patterns::Singleton;

    Single * s = Single::getInstance();
    delete s;
}
```

Solution – The double checked locked pattern (DCLP)

In a multi-threaded environment it is mandatory to acquire a lock() before accessing the singleton instance for not incurring in risks of conflicts across threads. This is achieved by the first code snippet reported below: the solution is always correct but it needs to always perform an expensive lock. An optimization sometimes used is the so called double checked locked pattern (DCLP), which tests for the value being null before trying to acquire a lock. Some architectures can implement code optimizations and break the correctness of the solution. The interested reader can find more information in *"C++ and the Perils of Double-Checked Locking, Scott Meyers and Andrei Alexandrescu, 2004"*

Code

```
Singleton* Singleton::instance() {
    Lock lock; // acquire lock
    if (pInstance == 0) {
        pInstance = new Singleton;
    }
    return pInstance;
} // release lock (via Lock destructor)

Singleton* Singleton::instance() {
    if (pInstance == 0) { // 1st test
        Lock lock;
        if (pInstance == 0) { // 2nd test
            pInstance = new Singleton;
        }
    }
    return pInstance;
}
```

6. Implementing the Object pool pattern

Solution

The Object pool is a pattern used for caching objects and avoiding expensive re-creations. This pattern is frequently used for objects representing the connection to a database shared among multiple clients. For instance this pattern has been used for implementing java JDBC drivers.

In this simplified example we allocated a cache of three objects but decided to adopt a very naïve cache policy which always returns the first object in the cache. More sophisticate allocation strategies can be adopted according to different needs. Also, locking strategies should be adopted in a multi-thread environment.

Code

```cpp
namespace Object_Pool{

    // Object pools are used to manage the object caching.
    // A client with access to an Object pool can avoid
    // creating a new Objects by simply asking the pool
    // for one that has already been instantiated instead.

    static const int num_objects = 3;
    class Object_to_share{

    public:
        Object_to_share(){
            std::cout << "\tAn object to share" << std::endl;
        };
    };

    class Pool{

    public:
        Object_to_share * getObject(void){
            std::cout << "\tGetting object" << std::endl;
            return &(objpool_[0]);
        }

    private:
        // could allocate dynamically
        Object_to_share objpool_[num_objects];
    };
}; // end ObjectPool

void testObjectPool(){

    using namespace Creational_Patterns::Object_Pool;

    Object_to_share o;
    Pool p;
    p.setObject(&o);
    Object_to_share * ptr = p.getObject();
}
```

Structural Patterns

Structural patterns compose interfaces by leveraging inheritance. The composition of objects allows to create new functionalities, simplify interfaces, adapt heterogeneous objects, improve performances, and reduce complexity.

7. Implementing the Adapter pattern

Solution

The adapter patter is used to allow operations between classes with incompatible interfaces by means of an appropriate wrapper.

In this example the adapter class inherits publically a *DesideredInterface* and privately a *LegacyInterface. DesideredInterface* is implemented according to a pure virtual method which is implemented by the adapter to make the existing class work with others without modifying their source code. An alternative and more modern implementation driven by templates instead of private inheritance is also provided.

Code

```cpp
namespace Adapter{

    // The Adapter pattern allows otherwise incompatible
    // classes to work together by converting the interface
    // of one class into an interface expected by the
    // clients.

    class DesiredInterface{

    public:
        virtual void make() = 0;
    };

    class LegacyInterface{

    public:
        LegacyInterface() {
            std::cout << "\tCalled legacy" << std::endl;
        };
    };
    // privately inherits the legacy component
```

```cpp
class adapter : public DesiredInterface,
    private LegacyInterface{

public:
    adapter() : LegacyInterface(){};
    void make() {
        std::cout << "\tAdapter do something "
            << std::endl;
    }
};
}; //end adapter

void testAdapter()
{
    using namespace Structural_Patterns::Adapter;

    adapter * a = new adapter();
    a->make();
    delete a;
}


template<typename T>
struct GenericVehicleAdapter : VehicleInterface {
    GenericVehicleAdapter(T* x) : m(x) { }
    virtual void Run() { return m->Run(); }
    T* m;
};

void testTemplateAdapter() {
    Shuttle shuttle;
    GenericAdapter<Shuttle> vehiclelike(&shuttle);
}
```

8. Implementing the Bridge pattern

Solution

The bridge pattern decouples the abstraction from its concrete implementation. In this way they can evolve independently. Following this patter the class itself can be considered as on specific implementation, while it is more generically seen as an abstraction. In C++ this pattern is sometime confused with the PIMPL (private implementation). However there are differences. PIMPL is a way of hiding the implementation. This is in order to break compilation dependencies. The Bridge pattern on the other hand is a way of supporting multiple implementations.

In this example the class *bridge* has a pointer *bridge_imp* and the two illustrative subclasses *a* and *b* provide specific implementation by means of the *a_imp* and *b_impi* classes.

Code

```cpp
namespace Bridge{

//
// Decouple an abstraction from its implementation so that the
// two can vary independently. This is different from
// Adapter which makes unrelated classes work together.

    class BridgeImp{ // de-couple

    public:
        BridgeImp() {};

    protected:
        int my_data_;
    };

    class Bridge{

    public:
        Bridge() {};

    protected:
        BridgeImp * imp_;
    };
    class AImp : public BridgeImp{ // implementat. hierarchy

    public:
        AImp() { my_data_ = 1; }// what you need here
    };
    class A : public Bridge{ // hierarchy

    public:
        A(){
            imp_ = new AImp();
            std::cout << "\tcreated a" << std::endl;
        };
        ~A(){
```

```cpp
                delete imp_;
                std::cout << "\tdeleted a" << std::endl;
        }
    };
    class BImp : public BridgeImp{ // implement. hierarchy

    public:
        BImp() { my_data_ = 2; }; // what you need here
    };
    class B : public Bridge{ // hierarchy

    public:
        B() {
            imp_ = new BImp();
            std::cout << "\tcreated b" << std::endl;
        };
        ~B(){
            delete imp_;
            std::cout << "\tdeleted b" << std::endl;
        }
    };
}; // end Bridge

void testBridge()
{
    using namespace Structural_Patterns::Bridge;

    A bridgeA;
    B bridgeB;
}
```

9. Implementing the Composite pattern

Solution

The composite pattern is used to compose multiple objects with common behaviour in such a way that they can be operated as one single object. A typical use is with a tree-like object composition.

In this example the *Component* class is implemented according to a pure virtual method traverse, which is implemented at its turn by the subclass *Leaf* and by the subclass *Composite.* In addition *Composite* maintains a vector of pointers where *Components* are inserted. This vector is used to iterate the whole structure.

Code

```cpp
namespace Composite{

    // Compose objects into tree structures to represent
    // whole-part hierarchies. Recursive composition

    class Component{

    public:
        virtual void traverse() = 0;  // pure virtual
    };


    class Leaf : public Component{

    private:
        int value_; // whatever you need here

    public:
        Leaf(int val) : value_(val) {};
        void traverse() { std::cout << value_ << " "; }
    };

    class Composite : public Component{

    private:
        std::vector< Component * > children_;
        typedef std::vector< Component * >::const_iterator
comp_const_it;

    public:
        void add(Component * e) { children_.push_back(e); };

        void traverse()
        {
            comp_const_it it = children_.begin();
            comp_const_it it_end = children_.end();
            for (; it != it_end; ++it)
                (*it)->traverse();
        }
    };

}; // end composite

void testComposite(){

    using namespace Structural_Patterns::Composite;
```

```
    Leaf l1(1);
    Leaf l2(2);
    Composite c;
    c.add(&l1); c.add(&l2);
    c.traverse();
}
```

10. Implementing the Decorator pattern

Solution

The decorator pattern is used to add additional behaviours to a method that is already existing for an object. In certain situations the existing behaviour is completely overridden. Those additional behaviours can be either permanent, or transient, or dynamically added at run-time.

In this example class A_and X inherit from A and implements the virtual method make() accordingly.

Code

```cpp
namespace Decorator{

    // Attach additional responsibilities to an object
    // dynamically. Decorators provide a flexible alternative
    // to subclassing for extending functionality.

    class A{

    public:
        A() { std::cout << "\tA" << std::endl; }

        virtual void make(void) {
            std::cout << "\t making A" << std::endl;
        }
    };
    // the decoration is private;

    class A_and_X : public A{

    public:
        void make(void) {
            A::make(); make_x();
        };
    private:
        void make_x() {
```

```
            std::cout << "\t making X" << std::endl;
        };
    };
}; // end Decorator
```

11.Implementing the Façade pattern

Solution

The façade pattern is used to provide a simplified interface to a large code segment so that the customers can only focus on the needed functionalities. This pattern is frequently used to reduce external code dependencies on the inner details of a library.

In this example three classes A, B, C are wrapped by one only class *façade* which simplifies the access to all former classes.

Code

```
namespace Facade{

    // "facade" object that provides a single, simplified
    // interface to the many individual interfaces within
    // the subsystem.

    class A{
    public:
        A() { std::cout << "\tInit A" << std::endl; }
        void make() { std::cout << "\tmake A" << std::endl; }
    };
    class B{
    public:
        B() { std::cout << "\tInit B" << std::endl; }
        void make() { std::cout << "\tmake B" << std::endl; }
    };
    class C{
    public:
        C() { std::cout << "\tInit C" << std::endl; }
        void make() { std::cout << "\tmake C" << std::endl; }
    };

    Class Facade{
    public:
        Facade() { a_.make(); b_.make(); c_.make(); }
    private:
        A a_;
```

```
            B b_;
            C c_;
    };
}; //end facade

void testFacade(){

    using namespace Structural_Patterns::Facade;
    Facade f;
}
```

12.Implementing the Flyweight pattern

Solution

The flyweight pattern is used for reducing the costs of creating a large number of similar objects. This is particularly important in those situations where performance is critical.

In this example *Icon* is a lightweight class which is stored in a vector contained within the *FlyweightFactory.* In this way a specific icon is nothing but a pointer to a specific object shared by every single instance of the same icon used by the windows system.

Code

```
namespace Flyweight{

    //The Flyweight pattern shares objects and reduce costs
    // in terms of memory and increase performance
    //
    // Clients should not instantiate Flyweights directly,
    // they should obtain them exclusively from a
    // FlyweightFactory object to shar properly.

    class Icon { // don't have a "huge" object for each Icon

    public:
        Icon(unsigned int i) : shared_name_(i) {};
        unsigned int getName(){ return shared_name_; }

    private:
        unsigned int shared_name_;
    };

    class FlyweightFactory{
```

```cpp
    public:
        static Icon * getIcon(unsigned int name)
        {
            std::vector<Icon *>::const_iterator it, it_end;
            it = icons_.begin();
            it_end = icons_.end();
            for (; it != it_end; ++it){
                if ((*it)->getName() == name){
                    std::cout <<
                    "\tFlyweight -> reusing an icon with name="
                        << name << std::endl;
                    return *it;
                }
            }
            icons_.push_back(new Icon(name));
            std::cout <<
                "\tCreated a new icon with name="
                << name << std::endl;
            return icons_.back();
        }; // an example: get an Icon allocated

        ~FlyweightFactory()
        {
            std::vector<Icon *>::const_iterator it, it_end;
            it = icons_.begin();
            it_end = icons_.end();
            for (; it != it_end; ++it){
                delete *it;
            }
        }

        private:
            static std::vector<Icon *>icons_;
        };

        std::vector<Icon *> FlyweightFactory::icons_;
        // force allocation
}; // end Flyweight


void testFlyweight(){

    using namespace Structural_Patterns::Flyweight;
    FlyweightFactory * fw = new FlyweightFactory();

    fw->getIcon(0);
    fw->getIcon(0);
```

```
        delete fw;
}
```

13.Implementing the Proxy pattern
Solution

The proxy pattern is used for mediating the access to an object in those situations where a need of additional functionalities is present. Those include, but are not limited to, control of access, reduction of complexity for operation, network access, access to a file system or to a large chunk on memory and more in general access to resources.

In this example an *ImageProxy* class is used to access an image which could be for instance located in a remote file system.

Code

```cpp
namespace Proxy{

    // The Proxy provides a surrogate to provide access to
    // an object. Example: A check or bank draft is a proxy
    // for funds in an account.

    // Decorator and Proxy have different purposes
    // but similar structures. Both describe how to provide
    // a level of indirection to another object,
    // and the implementations keep a reference to the object
    // to which they forward requests (delegation)

    class ImageProxy{

    private:
        unsigned int name_;

    public:
        ImageProxy(unsigned int name) : name_(name)
        {
            std::cout << "\tCreating image name="
                << name_ << std::endl;
        };

        ~ImageProxy()
        {
            std::cout << "\tDelete image name="
```

```cpp
                    << name_ << std::endl;
        };


        void draw()
        {
            std::cout << "\tDraw image name="
                << name_ << std::endl;
        };
    };

    class Image{

    private:
        ImageProxy * img_proxy_;
        static unsigned int name_;

    public:
        Image() : img_proxy_(0) {};
        ~Image() { delete img_proxy_; };

        void draw()
        {
            if (!img_proxy_)
                img_proxy_ =
                new ImageProxy(name_++);

            img_proxy_->draw();
        }
    };
    // this is used only for example
    unsigned int Image::name_ = 0;

}; // end Proxy

void testProxy()
{
    using namespace Structural_Patterns::Proxy;
    Image img;
    img.draw();

}
```

Behavioural Patterns

Behavioural patterns are used to describe interaction and communication among objects. Behavioural patterns are also used to handle the internal state and the internal activities of each object.

14. Implementing the Chain of responsibility pattern

Solution

A chain of responsibility pattern delegates a sequence of commands to a chain of processing objects. Objects can be dynamically added to a list.

In this example a *Base* class maintains a list of objects Base. Derived classes can register themselves and they can also provide specific *handle()* for detailed information.

Code

```cpp
namespace Chain_Of_Responsability{

    // Decoupling the sender of a request and its receiver
    // It gives more than one object a chance to handle
    // the request

    class Base
    {
    public:
        Base(unsigned int name) : name_(name), next_(0) {};
        void add(Base* n)  // add to the chain
        {
            if (next_)
                n->setPointer(next_);
            next_ = n;
        }
        void setPointer(Base * p) { next_ = p; }

        virtual void handle(unsigned int who){

            if (who == name_)
                std::cout << "\t" << name_ << " is the one"
                << std::endl;
            if (next_)
                next_->handle(who);
        }
```

```cpp
protected:
    unsigned int name_;

private:
    Base * next_;
};


class H1 : public Base{

public:
    H1(unsigned int name) : Base(name) {  };

    void handle(unsigned int who){
        std::cout << "\tHandler H1" << std::endl;
        Base::handle(who);
    }
};

class H2 : public Base{

public:
    H2(unsigned int name) : Base(name) {  };

    void handle(unsigned int who){
        std::cout << "\tHandler H2" << std::endl;
        Base::handle(who);
    }
};
}; // end Chain_Of_Responsability

void testChainOfResponsability(){

    using namespace
Behavioural_Patterns::Chain_Of_Responsability;

    H2 h2(2);
    H1 h1(1);
    Base b(0);

    b.add(&h1);
    b.add(&h2);
    h2.handle(2);
}
```

15.Implementing the Command pattern

Solution

The command pattern is used to create objects which encapsulate behaviours and states. This pattern is frequently needed when we want to delegate a sequence of calls with no need of explicitly knowing the parameter details or the specific methods here involved.

In this example the class *command* has a constructor which is initialized with the name of the *Person* and the particular commands used, which are *talk()* and *listen()*.

Code

```cpp
namespace Command{

    // Command decouples the object that invokes the
    // operation from the one that knows how to
    // perform it.
    class Person;

    class Command
    {
    private:
        Person *object_;
        void(Person:: *method_)();
    public:
        Command(Person *o = 0, void(Person:: *m)() = 0) :
            object_(o), method_(m)
        { }

        void execute()
        {
            (object_->*method_)();
        }
    };

    class Person
    {
    private:
        std::string name_;
        Command cmd_;
    public:
        Person(std::string n, Command c) : name_(n), cmd_(c)
        {}
```

```cpp
        void talk()
        {
            std::cout << name_ << " is talking" << std::endl;
            cmd_.execute();
        }
        void listen()
        {
            std::cout << name_ << " is listening" <<
             std::endl;
        }
    };
}; // end command

void testCommand()
{
    using namespace Behavioural_Patterns::Command;
    Person Angela("angela", Command());
    Person Willy("willy", Command(&Angela, &Person::listen));
    Willy.talk();
}
```

16.Implementing the Interpreter pattern

Solution

The Interpreter is a pattern used for implementing a specialized *interpreted* language. The idea is to have a class for each symbol of the grammar, used for defining the Interpreter.

In this example language is very simple and the input is taken from a stream of characters.

Code

```cpp
namespace Interpreter{

    class Interpreter
    {
    public:
        template<typename itr>
        static void runInterpreter(itr from, itr to)
        {
            for (itr i = from; i != to; ++i)
            {
                switch (*i)
                {
```

```cpp
                case 'h':
                    std::cout << "Hello";
                    break;
                case 'w':
                    std::cout << "world";
                    break;
                case ' ':
                    std::cout << ' ';
                    break;
                case 'n':
                    std::cout << endl;
                    break;
                default:
                    std::cout << "Unknown command";
                }
            }
        }
    };
};
```

17.Implementing the Iterator pattern

Solution

The Iterator pattern is used to access all the elements of an object without exposing its internal representation. This pattern is commonly used by libraries of containers such as the STL for decoupling accesses to a specific container from its implementation.

In this example a *stack* class is accessed by means of an iterator.

Code

```cpp
namespace Iterator{

    // An aggregate object such as a list should give you
    // a way to access its elements without exposing its
    // internal structure.

    class Stack
    {
    private:
        int items_[100];  // should be dynamic
        int sp_;          // current item

    public:
```

```cpp
        friend class Iterator; // friend it to access
iterator
        Stack() { sp_ = -1; }

        void push(int in) { items_[++sp_] = in; }
        int pop() { return items_[sp_--]; }
        bool isEmpty() { return (sp_ == -1); }
    };

    class Iterator{

    private:
        const Stack &stk_;   // access the structure
        int index_;

    public:
        Iterator(const Stack &s) : stk_(s), index_(0)
        {}       // initialize the iterator

        void operator++()
        {
            ++index_;
        }

        bool operator()()  // get the end of structure
        {
            return index_ != stk_.sp_ + 1;
        }

        int operator *()
        {
            return stk_.items_[index_];
        }
    };

    bool operator == (const Stack &s1,
        const Stack &s2)
    {
        Iterator it1(s1), it2(s2);

        for (; it1(); ++it1, ++it2)
        if (*it1 != *it2)
            return false;

        return true;
    }
}; // end Iterator
```

```cpp
void testIterator()
{
    using namespace Behavioural_Patterns::Iterator;
    Stack s;
    Iterator it(s);
    s.push(10);
    s.push(20);

    while (it())
    {
        std::cout << *it << ' ';
        it++;
    }
}
```

It is worth noting that in C++ iterators are frequently implemented by using the semantic of pointers with classical operations of deference, increment, decrement and pointer comparison for indicating when the end of the container has been reached. We have already used iterators for instance in this code snippet

```cpp
std::vector<Icon *>::const_iterator it, it_end;
it = icons_.begin();
it_end = icons_.end();
for (; it != it_end; ++it){
    if ((*it)->getName() == name){
        std::cout <<
        "\tFlyweight -> reusing an icon="
            << name << std::endl;
        return *it;
    }
}
```

18.Implementing the Mediator pattern

Solution

The Mediator allows interactions among classes with loose coupling. Each class is not required to recognize too much details of the other classes logic, which is exposed only to the mediator. Objects are not required to communicate directly anymore but they leverage the mediator, thereby reducing the coupling effects.

In this example the class *list* acts as a mediator among *nodes.*

Code

```
namespace Mediator{

    // Define an object that encapsulates how a set
    // of objects interact. promotes loose coupling
    //
    // for example a list mediates between node objects

    class Node {

    private:
        int v_;

    public:
        Node(int v) : v_(v){};
        int getValue() { return v_; }
    };

    class List { // mediating nodes

    private:
        std::vector<Node *> values_;
        typedef std::vector<Node *>::const_iterator const_it;

    public:
        void add(Node *n){ values_.push_back(n); }
        void traverse()
        {
            const_it it1 = values_.begin();
            const_it it2 = values_.end();
            for (; it1 != it2; it1++)
                std::cout << " " << (*it1)->getValue();
            std::cout << std::endl;
        }
    };
}; // end mediator

void testMediator()
{
    using namespace Behavioural_Patterns::Mediator;

    Node n1(1), n2(2), n3(3);
    List l; l.add(&n1); l.add(&n2); l.add(&n3);
    l.traverse();
}
```

19.Implementing the Memento pattern

Solution

Memento is a patter used to store and restore the state of an object. This is generally used for supporting undo operations, for supporting serialization, or for storing the seed of a pseudorandom number generator.

In this example a class *memento* is used to store a value which is saved and successively restored by the class *client.* More sophisticate implementations can use a vector to store multiple values and support 'undo' operations.

Code

```cpp
namespace Memento{

    // The client requests a Memento from the source object
    // when it needs to checkpoint the source object's state
    // If the client subsequently needs to "rollback" the
    // source object's state, it hands the Memento back to
    // the source object for reinstatement.

    class Memento{

    public:
        Memento(int val) : value_(val) {};
        int getValue() { return value_; };
    private:
        friend class Client;
        int value_;
    };

    class Client{ // client

    public:
        Client(int value) : value_(value) {};
        void increment() { ++value_; } // change of state;
        int get_value() { return value_; }

        Memento * create_memento() {
            return new Memento(value_);
        }
        void restore_from_memento(Memento * m) {
            value_ = m->value_;
```

```
        }

    private:
        int value_;

    };

}; // end memento

void testMemento()
{
    using namespace Behavioural_Patterns::Memento;

    Client c(20);
    Memento * m = c.create_memento();
    std::cout << m->getValue();
    delete m;
}
```

20.Implementing the Observer pattern

Solution

The Observer pattern implements the publisher/subscriber interactions, where a number of registered observer objects are informed about events produced by the publishers. This pattern is frequently used for implementing a distributed event handling system and for windows systems.

In this example the class *Observer* is implemented according to a pure virtual method *update* which is itself implemented by subclasses *a_observer* and *b_observer*. The class subject *keeps* a vector of observers which are notified by calling the method *notify()*. Note that new observers can be dynamically attached to existing lists.

Code

```
namespace Observer{

    // when one object changes state,
    // all its dependents are notified and
    // updated automatically.

    class Observ{
```

```cpp
public:
    virtual void update(int value) = 0;
};

class AObserv : public Observ{

public:
    void update(int value)
    {
        std::cout << "\ta seeing " <<
            value << std::endl;
    }
};

class BObserv : public Observ{

public:
    void update(int value)
    {
        std::cout << "\tb seeing " <<
            value << std::endl;
    }
};

class Subject{

private:
    int value_;
    std::vector<Observ *>  observers_;
    typedef std::vector<Observ *>::const_iterator
const_it;

public:
    void set_value(int value) {
        value_ = value; notify();
    }

    // attach the observers
    void attach(Observ * o) {
        observers_.push_back(o);
    }
    void notify()
    {
        const_it it = observers_.begin(),
            it_end = observers_.end();
        for (; it != it_end; ++it)
            (*it)->update(value_);
    }
```

```
    };
}; // end observer

void testObserver()
{
    using namespace Behavioural_Patterns::Observer;

    AObserv a;
    BObserv b;
    Subject s;

    s.attach(&a);    s.attach(&b);
    s.set_value(3);
}
```

21.Implementing the State pattern

Solution

The State pattern is used to allow an object to change his behaviour, when the internal state of the object itself is changing. For instance this pattern can be used to change the state of an object at run-time.

In this simple example the class state is implemented according to two virtual methods *on(..)* and *off(..)* which are at their turn implemented in the class OFF() and ON() respectively. The current state is maintained within the class *tool* as a pointer.

Code

```
namespace State {

    // Allow an object to alter its behavior when its
    // internal state changes. The object will appear
    // to change its class.

    class tool{

    private:
        class state * current_;

    public:
        void set_current(state * s) { current_ = s; };
        void on();
        void off();
    };
```

```cpp
class state{

public:
    virtual void on(tool * t){
        std::cout << " state on\n";
    }
    virtual void off(tool *t){
        std::cout << " state off\n";
    }
};

void tool::on()
{
    std::cout << "on is the state";
    current_->on(this);
}

void tool::off()
{
    std::cout << "off is the state";
    current_->off(this);
}

class OFF : public state{  // changing state OFF->on

public:
    void on(tool * t);
};

class ON : public state{  // changing state off->ON

public:
    void off(tool * t){

        std::cout << "\tgoing from ON to OFF" <<
        std::endl;
        t->set_current(new OFF());
        delete this;
    }
};

void OFF::on(tool * t){

    std::cout << "\tgoing from OFF to ON" << std::endl;
    t->set_current(new ON());
    delete this;
}
```

```cpp
}; // end State

void testState()
{
    using namespace Behavioural_Patterns::State;

    Tool * t = new Tool();
    ON * on = new ON();
    t->set_current(on);
    on->off(t);
    delete t;
}
```

22.Implementing the Strategy pattern

Solution

The Strategy pattern allows selection at run-time on specific algorithms for implementing a particular behaviour given a class of similar algorithms for that function.

In this example we have two classes *algo1* and *algo2* derived by the superclass *strategy*.

Code

```cpp
namespace Strategy{

    // Strategy lets the algorithm vary independently
    // from the clients that use it.

    enum ALGO { ALGO1, ALGO2 };

    class Strategic{

    public:
        virtual void do_it() = 0;
    };

    class Algo1 : public Strategic{

        void do_it() {
            std::cout << "\tcalling algo1" << std::endl;
        }
    };
```

```cpp
class Algo2 : public Strategic{

    void do_it() {
        std::cout << "\tcalling algo2" << std::endl;
    }
};


class Testbed{

public:

    Testbed() : strategy_(NULL) {};
    void choose_strategy(unsigned int what)
    {
        Strategic * tmp;

        switch (what){
        default:
        case ALGO1:
            tmp = new Algo1();
            delete strategy_;
            strategy_ = tmp;
            break;
        case ALGO2:
            tmp = new Algo2();
            delete strategy_;
            strategy_ = tmp;
            break;
        }
        strategy_->do_it();
    }

    ~Testbed(){
        if (strategy_)
            delete strategy_;
    }

private:
    Strategic * strategy_;
};
} // end Strategy

void testStrategy()
{
    using namespace Behavioural_Patterns::Strategy;
    Testbed tb;
```

```
        tb.choose_strategy(1);
}
```

23.Implementing the Template pattern

Solution

The template pattern allows the definition of algorithms skeleton as an abstract class, where subclasses have the responsibility of providing its concrete behaviour. The word template is not related to C++ templates.

In this example the class *algorithm_base* has 3 basic steps *a()*, *b()*, and *c()* and it is implemented according to two pure virtual methods *X()*, and *Y()* , which are then appropriately implemented by the two derived classes.

Code

```cpp
namespace Template{

    // Define the skeleton of an algorithm
    // deferring some steps to client subclasses

    class AlgorithmBase{

        void a() { std::cout << "\tA" << std::endl; }
        void b() { std::cout << "\tB" << std::endl; }
        void c() { std::cout << "\tC" << std::endl; }
        virtual void X() = 0;
        virtual void Y() = 0;

    public:

        void execute() { a(); X(); b();  Y(); c(); }
    };

    class AlgorithmRefinementFirstModel : public
AlgorithmBase{

        void X() { std::cout << "\tX1" << std::endl; }
        void Y() { std::cout << "\tY1" << std::endl; }
    };

    class AlgorithmRefinementSecondModel :public
AlgorithmBase{
```

```cpp
        void X() { std::cout << "\tX2" << std::endl; }
        void Y() { std::cout << "\tY2" << std::endl; }
    };

} // end Template

void testTemplate()
{
    using namespace Behavioural_Patterns::Template;
    AlgorithmBase * a = new AlgorithmRefinementFirstModel();
    a->execute();
    delete a;
    a = new AlgorithmRefinementSecondModel();
    a->execute();
    delete a;
}
```

24.Implementing the Visitor pattern

Solution

The Visitor pattern allows to visit an object in a hierarchical way with no need of considering internal details. In this way algorithms can be separated from the object structure on which they operate.

In this example the class *Parent* contains a vector of *parent_elements* pointers and a pure virtual method *accept()* which is then implemented by the subclasses. Two different implementations of parent visitors have been provided.

Code

```cpp
namespace Visitor{

    // Represent an operation to be performed on the elements
    // of an object structure.  Operations are performed
    // without polluting internal object

    // A practical result of this separation is the ability
    // to add new operations to existing object structures
    // without modifying those structures.

    // In essence, the visitor allows one to add new
    // virtual functions to a family of classes without
    // modifying the classes themselves;
```

```cpp
class A;
class B;
class C;
class Parent;

// an interface for visitor

struct parent_element_visitor{

    virtual void visit(A &a) const = 0;
    virtual void visit(B &b) const = 0;
    virtual void visit(C &c) const = 0;
    virtual void visit(Parent &p) const = 0;
    virtual ~parent_element_visitor() {};
};

// interface for a single element in hierarchy

struct parent_element{

    virtual void accept(const parent_element_visitor&
visitor) = 0;
    virtual ~parent_element() {};
};

// class in hierarchy

class A : public parent_element{

public:
    A() { std::cout << "\tcalled A" << std::endl; }

    void accept(const parent_element_visitor & v)
    {
        v.visit(*this);
    }
};

// class in hierarchy

class B : public parent_element{

public:
    B() { std::cout << "\tcalled B" << std::endl; }

    void accept(const parent_element_visitor & v)
    {
        v.visit(*this);
```

```cpp
    }
};

// class in hierarchy

class C : public parent_element{

public:
    C() { std::cout << "\tcalled C" << std::endl; }

    void accept(const parent_element_visitor & v)
    {
        v.visit(*this);
    }
};

// container of all the objects in hierarchy

class Parent{

public:
    typedef std::vector<parent_element*>::const_iterator
const_parent_collection_it;
    typedef std::vector<parent_element*>
parent_collection;

    parent_collection& getElements()
    {
        return elements_;
    }

    Parent()
    {
        elements_.push_back(new A());
        elements_.push_back(new B());
        elements_.push_back(new C());
    }
    ~Parent()
    {
        for (const_parent_collection_it it =
elements_.begin();
            it != elements_.end(); ++it)
        {
            delete *it;
        }                       // call the destructors
    }

private:
```

```cpp
        parent_collection elements_;
    };


    // a first concrete implementation of visitor

    class parent_model_one_visitor : public
parent_element_visitor{

    public:
        void visit(A &a) const {
            std::cout << "\tvisit A, model one"
                << std::endl;
        }
        void visit(B &b) const {
            std::cout << "\tvisit B, model one"
                << std::endl;
        }
        void visit(C &c) const {
            std::cout << "\tvisit B, model one"
                << std::endl;
        }

        void visit(Parent &p) const {

            Parent::parent_collection& elements =
                p.getElements();
            for (Parent::const_parent_collection_it it =
                elements.begin();
                it != elements.end(); ++it){

                // calling the visitor callback
                (*it)->accept(*this);
            };
        }
    };

    // a second concrete implementation of visitor

    class parent_model_two_visitor :
        public parent_element_visitor{

    public:
        void visit(A &a) const {
            std::cout << "\tvisit A, model two"
                << std::endl;
        }
        void visit(B &b) const {
```

```cpp
            std::cout << "\tvisit B, model two"
                << std::endl;
        }
        void visit(C &c) const {
            std::cout << "\tvisit B, model two"
                << std::endl;
        }

        void visit(Parent &p) const {

            Parent::parent_collection& elements =
                p.getElements();
            for (Parent::const_parent_collection_it it =
                elements.begin();
                it != elements.end(); ++it){

                // calling the visitor callback
                (*it)->accept(*this);
            };
        }
    };

};      // end visitor

void testVisitor()
{
    using namespace Behavioural_Patterns::Visitor;

    Parent p;
    parent_element_visitor * pv = new
parent_model_one_visitor();
    pv->visit(p);
    delete pv;
    pv = new parent_model_two_visitor();
    pv->visit(p);
    delete pv;
}
```

ABOUT THE AUTHOR

An experienced data mining engineer, passionate about technology and innovation in consumers' space. Interested in search and machine learning on massive dataset with a particular focus on query analysis, suggestions, entities, personalization, freshness and universal ranking. Antonio Gulli has worked in small startups, medium (Ask.com, Tiscali) and large corporations (Microsoft, RELX). His carrier path is about mixing industry with academic experience.

Antonio holds a Master Degree in Computer Science and a Master Degree in Engineering, and a Ph.D. in Computer Science. He founded two startups, one of them was one of the earliest search engine in Europe back in 1998. He filed more than 20 patents in search, machine learning and distributed system. Antonio wrote several books on algorithms and currently he serves as (Senior) Program Committee member in many international conferences. Antonio teaches also computer science and video game programming to hundreds of youngsters on a voluntary basis.

"Nowadays, you must have a great combination of research skills and a just-get-it-done attitude."

www.ingramcontent.com/pod-product-compliance
Lightning Source LLC
Chambersburg PA
CBHW041146050326
40689CB00001B/502